FINANCE 101 FOR KIDS

THE ABC OF

MONEY

BY
DIPO ADESINA
FAITHFUL ADESINA

Copyright Protection

MESSAGE FOR PARENTS

As a parent, it is important to teach your child about the value of money and the basics of financial management. Providing your child with a strong financial education is one of the most valuable gifts you can give them. It will equip them with the knowledge and skills they need to make sound financial decisions and set them up for a lifetime of financial success. This book will give them the foundation they need.

A is for
ASSETS

MEANING:

An asset is something that you own that has value and can put more money in your pocket or bank account.

EXAMPLE:

Champion was gifted a PlayStation 5 for his birthday, he now owns an asset. If his friends come to the house every weekend and pays him $5 to play, that means his asset is putting money into his pocket.

1

A is for
ASSETS

B is for
BUDGET

MEANING:

A budget is a plan for how you will use your money. It helps you decide what you should spend your money on and how much to spend.

EXAMPLE:

Greatness received $20 for her allowance. She decided to put away $5 for a barbie she wants to buy, another $5 to buy candy, and then save the remaining $10 for the future.

B is for
BUDGET

C is for
CASH FLOW

MEANING:

Cash flow is how money comes in and out of a person's account or business. It helps you to understand where your money is coming from and where it is going.

EXAMPLE:

Greatness received $20 for doing her chores, this is called inflow. She then goes to the store and spends the $10 she budgeted for her barbie and candy, this is called outflow.

C is for
CASH FLOW

D is for
DEBT

MEANING:

Debt is when someone owes money to someone else.

EXAMPLE:

Champion goes to his sister Greatness and asked her to borrow him $10. He wants to add it to his money to buy a game for his PlayStation 5. He promised to pay her back later. That $10 is a debt.

D is for
DEBT

E is for
EXPENSE

MEANING:

An expense is something that costs money. It is something that you need to pay for to live your life or run a business.

EXAMPLE:

Champion spends $3 in school every day to buy lunch. The lunch is an expense because he needs to eat in school.

E is for
EXPENSE

F is for
FIXED COST

MEANING:

Fixed cost is an expense that you pay for whether you use them or not.

EXAMPLE:

Champion likes to watch the Jurassic World Series on Netflix. He needs to pay $6.99 every month for Netflix, even if he is does not watch Jurassic World every day.

F is for
FIXED COST

G is for
GROSS INCOME

MEANING:

Gross income is the total amount of money that someone earns before other deductions are taken out, such as taxes.

EXAMPLE:

Greatness earns $20 per week for doing her chores. Her gross income is $20.

G is for
GROSS INCOME

H is for
HEDGE

MEANING:

Hedge is a way to protect yourself from losing money.

EXAMPLE:

Champion is afraid he will stop earning money if his game stops working, so he decided to buy a second game as a backup. That way, if the first game breaks, he will have another game for his friends to play with and he will continue to earn money.

15

H is for
HEDGE

I is for
INTEREST

MEANING:

Interest is a way for someone to earn more money in addition to the money they are lending to someone else.

EXAMPLE:

Greatness decides to give Champion the $10 he asked for under one condition. Champion must pay back the $10 with an additional $2, making the total amount he has to pay back $12. The $2 is considered interest.

17

I is for
INTEREST

J is for
JOB

MEANING:

A job is something that people do to earn money.

EXAMPLE:

When Greatness helps her neighbor to walk their dog three times a week, that is considered a job because that is something she does to earn money.

J is for
JOB

K is for
KNOW YOUR CUSTOMER

MEANING:

"Know your customer" (KYC) is a process that helps a business to understand who their customers are and what they need.

EXAMPLE:

Champion invites his friends to his house and asks them what type of video games they like, an action or a sport game? This helps Champion to know what his customers (friends) like, so he can buy the game and charge them $5 to play.

21

K is for
KNOW YOUR CUSTOMER

L is for
LIABILITY

MEANING:

A liability is something that a person or a business owes to someone else.

EXAMPLE:

Champion took the $10 from his sister to buy the game. The $10 is a liability because he owes his sister $10 plus the $2 interest. Once he pays her back, then he no longer has a liability.

L is for
LIABILITY

M is for
MONEY

MEANING:

Money is something that you use to pay for things that you need or want.

EXAMPLE:

The only way for Champion to buy the game he wanted was to give the store owner money in exchange for the game.

M is for MONEY

26

N is for
NET WORTH

MEANING:

Net worth is a way of knowing how much money and assets someone has. You subtract what they owe (debt/liability) other people from what they own (assets).

EXAMPLE:

Champion has a PlayStation 5 that is worth $400 and games worth $50. His total asset is $450. He owes his sister $12, so his net worth is $438. ($450 - $12=$438)

27

N is for
NET WORTH

O is for
OPPORTUNITY

MEANING:

An opportunity is a chance to do something that might be helpful, and also make more money for a business.

EXAMPLE:

Champion's friends often complain about not having snacks to munch on while playing the video game. He realized, that was an opportunity to make more money. He decided to start buying candy to resell to his friends.

29

O is for OPPORTUNITY

P is for
PASSIVE INCOME

MEANING:

Passive income is money that you earn without having to work for it.

EXAMPLE:

As long as Champion's friends come over to the house to play the video game, he will always earn $5 per person. The $5 is passive income because he is not doing anything to earn the money.

P is for
PASSIVE INCOME

Q is for QUOTATION

MEANING:

Quotation is a way to tell someone how much something will cost before they agree to buy it.

EXAMPLE:

Champion just made a new friend, Winner. He told Winner about his gaming business. Winner then asked, how much would it cost to play on Saturday and Sunday? Champion told him the two days will cost him $12. $5 for the game, and $1 for the candy each day.

Q is for
QUOTATION

R is for
REVENUE

MEANING:

Revenue is the money that a person or a business earns from selling products or services.

EXAMPLE:

After four weeks of running his gaming business, champion earned a total of $50 from his friends playing the video game and buying candy.

R is for
REVENUE

S is for
STOCK

MEANING:

A stock is a type of investment that makes you part of the owner of a company. When you buy a stock, you are buying a small piece of the company.

EXAMPLE:

Champion used some of his money to buy stock in the company that created PlayStation. If the company does well, his stock might make money. If the company does poorly, his stock might lose money.

37

S is for
STOCK

T is for
TAX

MEANING:

Tax is a fee that people and businesses must pay to the government.

EXAMPLE:

Champion needs to pay a portion of his money to the government. The government will use the money for things that benefits everyone. For example, building public schools, which allows kids to attend school for free.

39

T is for
TAX

U is for
UNSECURED DEBT

MEANING:

Unsecured debt is a type of debt that someone owes and promises to pay, even though they don't have assets that is worth the amount of debt they owe.

EXAMPLE:

Champion's friend asked him for $50 to buy a game, and promised to pay him back. He doesn't have anything he can give to Champion to sell just in case he is unable to pay back the money.

40

U is for
UNSECURED DEBT

V is for
VARIABLE COST

MEANING:

Variable cost is an expense that changes based on how much a business produces or sells.

EXAMPLE:

The cost of the candy Champion buys at the store for his friends is variable cost. If he has more friends over for the weekend, then he has to spend more money buying candy, but if he has less friends, he spends less money.

42

V is for
VARIABLE COST

W is for WALLET

MEANING:

A wallet is a small container that you can use to carry things like money.

EXAMPLE:

Champion keeps his money inside his wallet when he gets paid from his friends.

W is for
WALLET

X is for
XENOCURRENCY

MEANING:

Xenocurrency is any currency (money) that is used outside of the country where it was created.

EXAMPLE:

Champion's family decided to travel to Mexico for vacation. He was able to spend some of the money he earned from his video game business to buy something to eat and drink in Mexico.

46

X is for
XENOCURRENCY

Y is for YIELD

MEANING:

Yield is a way to find out how much a person or a business is earning in addition to the money they have.

EXAMPLE:

Champion decided that he no longer wants to keep all his money in his wallet, so his parents helped him to open a savings account where he earns 3% interest on the $50 he is saving for the year. That means his $50 will yield 3%, which is $1.5.

Y is for YIELD

Z is for
ZERO BALANCE ACCOUNT

MEANING:

A Zero Balance Account (ZBA) is a type of bank account that is linked to another account. You can later transfer money from the first account into the ZBA when you need to.

EXAMPLE:

Champion decided to open a separate account from his savings account. Champion will only transfer money from his savings account into the new account when he wants to buy a game.

50

Z is for
ZERO BALANCE ACCOUNT

Made in the USA
Middletown, DE
19 September 2024